How to Build an Indian Canoe

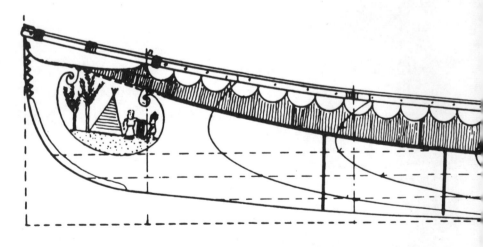

How to Build

David McKay Company, Inc.   New York

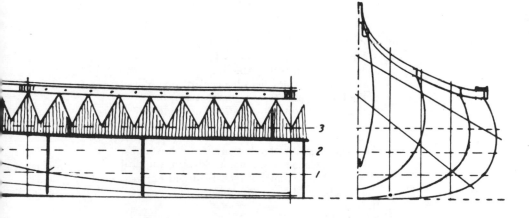

an Indian Canoe
adapted by George S. Fichter

Library of Congress Cataloging in Publication Data

Fichter, George S.
  How to build an Indian canoe.

  Adaptation of E. T. Adney's The bark canoes
and skin boats of North America.
  SUMMARY: Describes the construction of a canoe
as the Indians used to do it and discusses the
distinctive features of the craft of various tribes.
  1. Indians of North America—Boats—Juvenile
literature. 2. Canoes and canoeing—North America
—Juvenile literature. [1. Indians of North America
—Boats. 2. Canoes and canoeing—North America]
I. Adney, Edwin Tappan, 1868-1950. The bark canoes
and skin boats of North America.
II. Title.
E98.B6F52   970'.004'97   76-13252
ISBN 0-679-20352-4
10 9 8 7 6 5 4 3 2 1

Contents

Bark Canoes

1 Early explorers in the New World quickly recognized the bark canoes used by the Indians as one of their most valuable discoveries. Traveling in the wilderness was much faster and easier on the waterways, and these unusual canoes were far better suited for this purpose than were the wooden boats that the Europeans brought with them.

First of all, the bark canoes were astonishingly lightweight. Even a boat large enough to carry half a dozen men and their supplies weighed only about a hundred pounds itself. Weight was important to the explorers, for it was necessary to make many portages around rapids or waterfalls or from one stream to another.

Though they weighed little themselves, the canoes were both strong and stable. The larger canoes could be loaded with a ton of weight—men and supplies—but they were not easily capsized even in rough or fast waters.

Another advantage, the canoes were paddled rather than rowed. This meant that the men who supplied the power and also steered the craft faced the direction they were going. In the narrow, swift, and unknown waterways, this was important both for comfort and for safety. Because of their remarkable buoyancy, the bark canoes could skim through very shallow water.

Speed was also a great advantage of the bark canoes over the heavy, cumbersome wooden boats. In the North Country the summers were brief, and the fast canoes made it possible to travel long distances and be back home before winter set in. Fur traders made wide circuits through the wilderness to get loads of furs and then returned to trading posts before ice closed the waterways.

Compared to wooden boats, the bark canoes were fragile, true. But the canoes were made of materials abundant in the area. Repairs were not difficult and did not generally take much time.

Immediately the Europeans set about learning the art of making bark canoes. The Indians had obviously developed their skills over many generations and had long ago resolved whatever problems they may have had originally with designs and engineering. They made their canoes in sizes for from two to twenty or more men and for use on streams or in open water—even the sea. Some were designed for speed, others to haul heavy loads. The most famous were those made from the bark of the paper birch tree, but the Indians could make suitable canoes also from the bark of elms or other trees.

Each tribe built canoes of a distinctive design, as identifiable as their different languages. All the white man ever contributed was newer tools, for until the arrival of the Europeans, the Indians lived in the Stone Age, their implements made of stone, bone, and wood. In the factories the white men established for making bark canoes, procedures

Giant bark canoes, some as long as 36 feet, were used by Hudson Bay Company fur traders.

were somewhat streamlined, and canoes of very large size were built to carry heavier loads of furs. But the basic materials and techniques were learned from the Indians, and in these, improvements were not necessary.

No one knows how long ago the Indians learned the art of building bark canoes. That story is lost in tribal antiquity. Jacques Cartier, the French explorer, was the first European

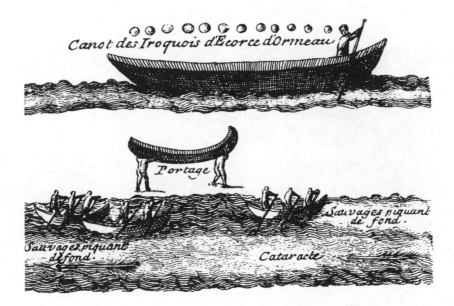

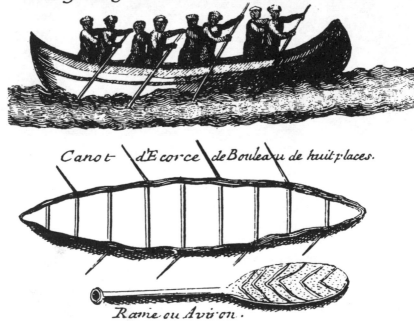

Early illustrations of bark canoes did not reveal details.

to report seeing bark canoes—in 1535. It was not until the early 1600s, however, that the logs of the explorers contained detailed descriptions of the craft—their design and workmanship—as well as comments about various sizes and speeds. But by this time both the French and the English were already using the canoes.

Birch Country

2 Bark canoes were built by the Indians of a dozen or more tribes, all of whom shared one thing in common: They lived in areas where the white or paper birch tree grew. This was a vast area of northern North America—virtually all of Canada and Alaska north to the cold, treeless tundra and extending southward through the northern tier of states from coast to coast in the United States. They grew most abundantly in the eastern portions of their extensive range, generally scattered among the pines, spruces, firs, maples, and other trees, but often forming dense thickets on rich, moist soils. Birches walled the banks of many streams. Occasionally they reached a height of 80 feet but were usually not taller than 40 or 50 feet. Paper birches produced numerous nutlets—as many as 4 million to the pound and each tree yielding many pounds. The birches spread quickly and invaded every possible hospitable grow-

The thin, tough bark of the paper, or white, birch was favored for building bark canoes.

ing site. Individuals did not live long compared to other trees. They rarely reached an age of 100.

Paper birch trees were prized for their tough, thin, smooth, chalky white bark, marked with dark or black horizontal lines. On the lower portions of the trunks—to about the height of the deep winter snows—the bark was rough and generally blemished. Above this, to the level of the lower limbs, it was well formed and had few blemishes. From the white outer bark to the greenish rind surrounding the wood, the bark peeled off in a series of buff to tan layers, each with the same horizontal lines as on the outer bark.

The Indians selected their trees carefully. The height of the tree did not always indicate thicker bark, and the quality of the bark might vary even in trees growing next to each

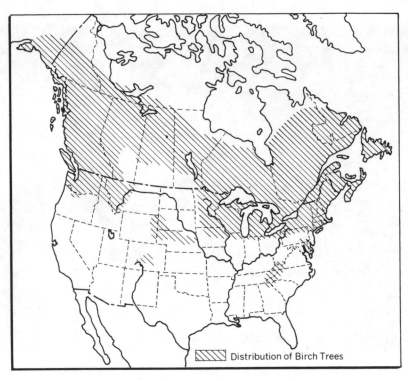

The North Country range of the paper birch.

other. Experience helped, especially in eliminating those that would yield bark with too many blemishes—"eyes" too large and close together, for example, which would cause the bark to split easily. To get large enough pieces of bark, only trees with long, straight trunks of uniform diameter were chosen, of course, but even with careful selection there was no sure way of knowing exactly what the bark would be like until it was peeled from the tree.

During the warm months, when the sap was flowing in the trees, the bark could be peeled from the tree easily. In winter, when the outside of the tree was frozen, it was possible to peel the bark only by heating the tree, i.e., building fires around it. After thaws in winter or in late spring or early fall, the bark could be peeled without use of heat, and it came off all the way down to the green rind—the tree's growing layer. The Indians called bark removed down to the rind "winter bark," even if it was taken off in this manner in the warmer months. The green rind first turned orange-red and then later became a rich, dark brown. Because the Indians put the white outer bark inside their canoes and used this innermost layer for the outside, the rind could later be scraped away, leaving only the designs that were desired. This was one of the reasons the Indians especially prized the winter bark. Poor-quality bark separated into its layers too easily and was rejected. Often the bark taken off in summer did this.

To peel the bark, a longitudinal or vertical cut or slash was made as far along the length of the trunk as desired. An edge of the bark was pried up with a stick, wedge, or knife and then was carefully pulled away from the trunk. The bark was handled with great care to keep it from splitting along the grain. Sometimes hot water was poured on the bark to keep it flexible even as it was being peeled. Sheets of bark peeled from the tree were rolled, and unless they were to be used immediately, they were submerged in water to prevent them from drying out.

Birch bark not only could be obtained in large sheets but also could be sewed together more easily than other kinds of bark. Its grain goes around the tree or is horizontal rather than running vertically along its length. Compared to other barks, it does not stretch or shrink; and while it is still green, or if kept wet, it remains elastic enough for pulling into a tight fit. When allowed to dry in the air and sun, it then becomes permanently taut over its framework.

But the bark of other trees was used to a limited degree. Several other kinds of birches grew in the same region, but they had a thinner bark of poorer quality. The bark of elms, hickories, chestnuts, cottonwoods, spruces, and several other trees was used occasionally and was good in emergencies or

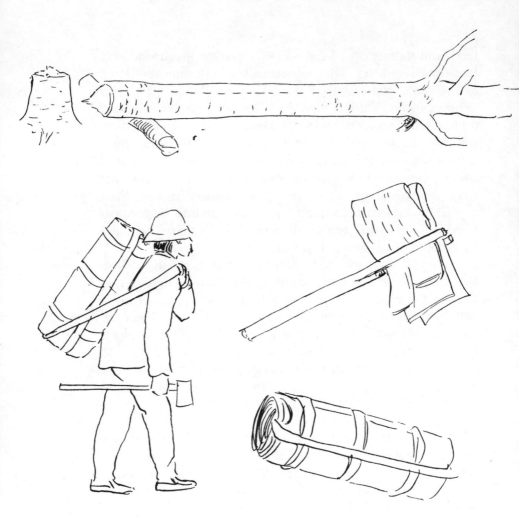

Peeling, rolling, and transporting bark for use in canoe construction.

for making canoes that were not expected to last long. Almost all had much rougher surfaces, and they had to be scraped to make them flexible. They could not be obtained in large sheets, and so a number of small ones had to be pieced together. Because they would shrink when dry and stretch when wet, they did not make a tight covering, and since they contained resins in large amounts, they could not be stored long ahead of time as could birch bark.

Where the paper birch grew, the art of making bark canoes flourished. This was the land of the Micmac, Malecite, St. Francis-Abnaki, and Beothuk in the Maritime Provinces of Canada. The Indians of all these tribes were experts. Central Canada also had canoe builders, most of them from the Algonkin family—the Eastern Cree, Têtes de Boule, Algonkins, Ojibway, and Western Cree. In northwestern Canada, the Chipewyan, Beaver, Nahane, Sekani, Kutenai, Salish, and others—mostly of the Athabascan family—were also bark canoe builders. The fur traders borrowed from various tribes but primarily from the Algonkins and the Ojibway to build their famous big canoes, also called *rabeskas,* or *maître canots,* that carried them through the North Country during their nearly two centuries of exploitation.

Materials and Tools

3 Birch bark was the primary ingredient of the Indian bark canoes, but other materials were needed, too. These could be varied, however, to utilize the best of what was available locally.

For lacing or sewing pieces of bark together, the Indians generally used roots of black spruce, which grew in the same region as the paper birch. The roots were long, slender (seldom larger in diameter than a lead pencil), and tough. They were remarkably durable, lasting as long as the canoe itself with ordinary wear, and while still green, or if kept wet, they were flexible enough so that lacings could be put close together and then pulled tight. Black spruce grew in soft, moist ground, the sought-after roots close to the surface. They were easily dug up either by hand or with a stick, and it was not uncommon to get a slim root that was as much as

Ojibway carrying bundle of spruce roots for use in sewing.

twenty feet long. As soon as the roots were gathered, they were split into strands of a suitable size and then stored in water to keep them flexible. Sometimes they were put in boiling water just before being used to soften them even more. The roots of other spruces, tamaracks, larches, and even pines were turned to if necessary, but all were inferior to those of the black spruce. Some tribes also used rawhide for lacings.

For sealing seams to make them watertight, the Indians used gum either from black or white spruce. Sometimes it could be collected from a tree that had fallen or was damaged, but often the Indians got the gum by making a slash in a tree in the spring and then collecting the gum that oozed out of the wound during the warm months. When it was time to use the gum, it was heated in a wooden trough or a stone or clay crock. After the arrival of the white man, metal kettles were used. The gum melts at a low temperature. Sometimes water was boiled and the gum was dropped into it. Since it floated on the surface when melted, it was easily skimmed off, and at the same time, bits of bark or other debris could be removed.

The melted gum was tempered by adding a bit of animal fat and finely powdered charcoal before it was used. This was tested by dipping a strip of bark into the melted gum and then quickly putting the coated bark in cold water. If the gum cracked when the piece of bark was bent, too much fat and charcoal had been added. More gum was then melted to dilute the mixture. If the gum did not crack, the piece of bark was held in the hand until it was completely cool and then was rubbed with the hand. If the gum was still tacky, or if it rolled off the strip, more tempering was needed.

Tempering was an important and tedious job. Sometimes the gum was remelted many times to get it just right for

Bow drill with stone awl for making holes in wood and bark.

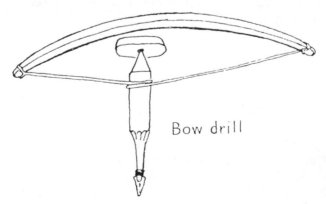

Bow drill

Stone wedge

Stone axe

Stone knife with rawhide
thong handle

Stone hammer

Wooden mauls

Stone scraper

Indians worked with Stone Age tools.

Steel canoe awls

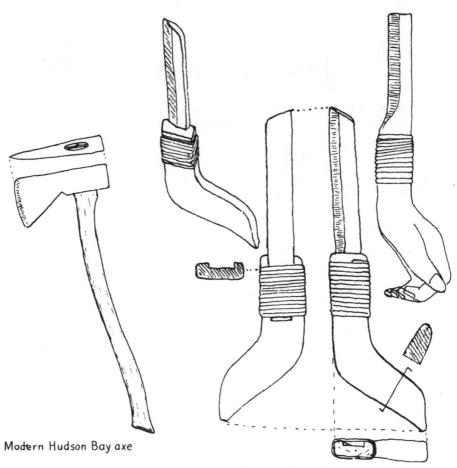

Modern Hudson Bay axe

Crooked knives

Steel tools introduced by the Europeans.

use. Each time it was melted, the gum became harder and darker. Most of the Indians used gum that was almost black, but some added dyes to give the final product a different and distinctive color.

Wood was also needed for the ribs, crosspieces or thwarts, gunwales, end pieces, and the sheathing (flooring and siding). Northern white cedar was preferred because it was strong and split cleanly when seasoned. Black spruce was used, too, but it split well only when green. Hard maple was a favorite for the crosspieces and also for paddles. Both white and black ash, larches, and pines were used occasionally, the Indians always resorting to the best of what could be obtained locally.

Before the arrival of the white man, the Indians had only primitive tools fashioned from stones, bones, shells, or pieces of wood. Today we can only marvel at the craftmanship accomplished with these crude and inefficient implements.

To cut a tree, the Indians combined fire with their stone axes or hatchets. Near the base of the tree they cut through the outer bark and loosened the fibers, girdling the tree. Above this cut they coated the tree with mud or clay to protect it, and then they built a fire to burn away and char the loosened wood. When the fire died down, they chipped away the char to expose more wood, then cut into the freshly exposed wood as much as possible and built another fire. This was repeated as many times as necessary until the tree finally fell. Using the same method, the fallen tree was cut into as many sections as desired. With fire and stone axes, the Indians could also make wedges or put sharp points on stakes.

The stone tools used by the Indians were chipped from flint, jasper, chalcedony, or other quartz rocks, one stone struck against another to knock off bumps and to make sharp edges. To make a really useful hammer, hatchet, knife, or wedge required skill, experience, and much patience. Some Indians did their work only when the rock was at a particular temperature, or they kept the rocks damp while they were being worked on to make as certain as possible that they flaked properly. Some stones were too brittle, but others could be sharpened to a degree by rubbing their cutting edges against a harder rock. None were ever superior tools for cutting or chopping. The tools were fastened to a stone handle and commonly wrapped with rawhide to give them a reasonably comfortable grip. Others, such as stone scrapers, were simply held in the hand.

Drilling was done with bone awls fashioned from splinters of bone from the leg bones of deer or other animals. These were either set in a wooden handle or were wrapped with rawhide to give them a firm grip. In canoe building, it was necessary to make holes in the bark for lacing or sewing and also to drill holes in some pieces of wood. For making large holes in hard wood, the awl was rotated back and forth with a bow drill, the awl itself steadied with a block that was held in the other hand. Some Indians rotated the awl between the palms of their hands and held the block of wood in their mouths to steady the awl.

With a stone knife, a shell, or the fingernails, the bark was peeled from the roots to be used for sewing, and then they were split into small strands. Sometimes the splitting was started by chewing on the root, or it could be battered between two rocks. Once the split was started, the root was rather easily pulled apart. One end was held in the mouth while the root was pulled away with the right hand. The thumb of the left hand was used as a guide to make certain the split was even. If the split began to go out of line, the root was bent to guide the splitting back on course again.

The pieces of wood to be used for the ribs, crosspieces, and sheathing were split with a stone wedge or with the edge

 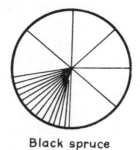

White cedar   Black spruce

Techniques for splitting two different kinds of wood.

of a knife or a hatchet. The blades were started into the wood by hitting them with a wooden maul. When a split was started, more wedges were driven in along the split until the wood was completely divided. Commonly the wood was first quartered and then each quarter split into smaller pieces. In white cedar, the splits were made parallel to the bark side, as this wood bends well only toward or away from the outer or bark side. Black spruce, in contrast, was split in the opposite direction, that is, with the broad side of the pieces away from the bark. Black spruce would not split easily in any other direction, and this was also the way it bent properly. Longer pieces were split in the same manner, but careful attention had to be given the selection of the piece of wood.

After the wood was split, the pieces were cut to proper lengths with a stone knife drawn back and forth like a saw. This process was very slow, but there was no other way. The wood was smoothed with stone scrapers or with sandstone and was then polished by rubbing it with a larger piece of wood or with fine sand held in a hide pad.

For the ribs and ends, the pieces of wood had to be bent. In a basin—usually a wooden trough—water was heated to boiling by dropping in hot stones. These were lifted from the fire with tongs made of green saplings. After the wood was thoroughly soaked in the hot water, the bending was started. More boiling water was poured over the wood during the bending process. As soon as the desired bend was obtained, thongs were tied to the ends to hold the wood in place until it dried. Very sharp bends, as in the stem or end pieces, were achieved by splitting the wood into thinner laminations in the area where the bend had to be greatest. When the bending was completed, these split areas were wrapped tightly with rawhide or roots.

Canoe building became many times faster when the white man brought steel tools. Axes, bucksaws, awls, wedges—all made the work easier, though they did not improve the workmanship. With the steel tools, it was possible, however, to remove bark more easily in large sheets, so that frequently only one or two pieces were needed for an entire canoe. In earlier days, often many pieces had to be used. The Indians especially liked the froe, a splitting tool consisting of a steel blade about 1½ feet long and 2 inches wide. One end had a loop in which a hardwood handle was set at right angles to the blade, its cutting edge directed down when the handle was up. The froe was driven into a piece of wood to be split by striking the quarter-inch-thick back of the blade with a maul. As soon as the split was started, one hand held the handle while the other was placed at the opposite end of the blade as the froe was pushed down with a wobbling, wiggling motion to force it through the wood and complete the split.

Perhaps most popular was the crooked knife, made from a flat steel file with one side reduced to a cutting edge. The end of the file was driven into a crotched stick and secured in place with rawhide (in later days, wire). The knife was held with the cutting edge toward the user, the fingers of one hand laid along the handle to help steady the blade. The knife was

The shaving horse for holding wood. Basic structure above; man shown at work on a shaving horse below.

drawn slowly toward the user to make the desired cuts for shaving the wood into whatever shape was needed.

Workers often sat at a so-called shaving horse. This was a four-legged bench about 7 feet long. A short, wedge-shaped piece of wood was fastened to its top. One end was beveled to hold it directly against the bench, and the other was lifted off the bench by a brace of wood about a foot high. A slot was cut through the bench and also through the slanted piece of wood fastened to the top. Through this slot a flat arm was extended; it was crooked at the top so that it overhung the slot. On the bottom of the arm were two foot rests. To use the bench, the worker sat facing the high end of the piece of wood fastened to the top, and he put his feet on the rests on the vertical arm. The piece of wood to be worked on was slipped between the arm and the slanted board, and the worker then pushed down with his feet to clamp it firmly in position. Both hands were free to use a crooked knife or a drawknife for shaping the wood.

Nails were among the last of the items to be adopted by the Indians in building their canoes, but eventually they were used to fasten the bark to the gunwales and, if one was used, to put a cap or top piece on the gunwale.

Constructing the Canoe

4 The Indians built canoes of various sizes and types or models, but the basic methods of construction were the same. The canoe described here in detail is of the Malecite type and is 19 feet long with a 3-foot beam. Specific differences in the canoes of different types are described later.

How did the Indians measure the size of the pieces of wood or bark needed? Some of the canoe builders had measuring sticks that helped. One stick was for half the length of the gunwale frame. Notches on the stick showed where the gunwales were lashed and also the position of each crosspiece, or thwart. A second stick was notched at half the length of each crosspiece, and notches on a third stick indicated the height of the gunwale at each crosspiece and at the ends—four notches in all for each half of the canoe. This measurement was from the bottom of the building bed, not

An Indian canoe-building site with a completed canoe in background and another framed on building bed. An unrolled piece of bark in foreground is held flat with rocks.

from the base line of the canoe. These sticks provided all the critical measurements needed for building a canoe of a particular size. Each different size or model required a different set of sticks.

Some Indians also used another system of measurement—less accurate but somewhat more convenient since it involved only parts of the body. One distance was from fingertips to fingertips with the arms outstretched. The English fur traders called this length the fathom, but it averaged about 64 inches, a bit less than the standard 72-inch nautical fathom. Another measurement was the greatest width of the ball of the thumb, which is about one inch. Others were the width of the four fingers of the hand held close together, or roughly three inches, and the length of the forearm to the knuckles of the clenched fist, about 15 inches. The disadvantage of this system was not only the variation from one person to another but also that these measurements were not related specifically to canoes. They had to be memorized and then applied to the particular size or model of canoe to be built.

The Indians needed the measurements necessary for building a properly proportioned canoe. Generally they measured the length of the canoe at the gunwales only, not the overall length as given for canoes today. Including the end pieces might actually add a foot or more to the total length. The width was measured inside the gunwales. If the sides bulged below the gunwales, this width might in fact be six inches or more greater. For building, depth was measured from the building bed to the bottom of the gunwale, as in the measuring stick.

Building sites were selected with great care, the same place often used for generations. The ground where the canoe was to be set up had to be smooth, with no stones or roots that might damage the bark. The soil had to be firm enough to hold stakes used to frame the canoe. Shade was important to keep the bark from drying out. Because an entire family or sometimes several families were involved in the building, the site had to be suitable also for camping, with both food and water available.

The first step in building the Malecite canoe described here was to put the gunwales together to outline the canoe on the building bed. The gunwales, made of white cedar, measured about 1½ inches square at their midpoint. Their edges were smooth or rounded, and the bottom outside edge

In first stage, gunwales were outlined on building bed, held in place with stakes to get proper curvature. Temporary crosspieces were also inserted at this time.

was beveled. They were tapered at their squared-off ends to roughly half their measurement at the middle so the ends could be conveniently joined with another piece by wrapping with spruce roots but adding little or nothing to the overall thickness. At the very middle of each gunwale on the inside, a cut (½ x 2 inches) was made for mortising in the center crosspiece, or thwart. Made of hard maple, this crosspiece was 33 inches long, 3 inches wide, and about ¾ of an inch thick for most of its length, tapered at about 5 inches from each end to a thickness of ¼ inch and 2 inches wide—to fit the mortise hole in the gunwale. The edges of the crosspiece were smoothed and rounded. To hold it in place, holes were drilled through both the gunwale and the crosspiece, then a wooden peg inserted. Small holes were also drilled near the ends of the crosspiece for inserting roots to lash the crosspiece to the gunwale.

Next, the ends of the gunwale were pulled together. To get the proper bow or curvature, temporary crosspieces were inserted about midway between the center crosspiece and the ends, which were then fastened together with pegs and lashed tightly with roots. To make certain the gunwale wrappings were tight, some canoe builders also drove a thin wedge of wood between the gunwale ends.

Now four more crosspieces were added—at 33 inches and 66 inches from the center on each side. The first pair measured about 26 inches in length, the second 15¼ inches. The width, thickness, and tapering for the 26-inch crosspieces was the same as for the middle crosspiece. The 15½-inch crosspieces were basically about 4 inches wide but were worked down to a width of about 3 inches in a curved shape, the bow toward the canoe ends.

All through the process of fitting the crosspieces the alignment of the gunwales was constantly checked to maintain the proper symmetry throughout.

The assembled gunwales were laid on the smooth building bed, which was built up about an inch higher in the middle to assure having a straight bottom on the finished canoe. The frame was positioned carefully so that the center crosspiece was exactly over the highest point. It was then weighted down with pieces of flat wood and stones. Around the outside of the gunwale frame, stakes made of saplings split in half and from 3 to 4 feet long were driven into the ground in pairs opposite each other and about 2 feet apart. None was positioned directly opposite a crosspiece. Those at the extreme ends were about a foot apart and only about 1½ inches from their opposing neighbors. The flat side of each stake was toward the gunwale and only about an inch from it. Finally, two more pairs of stakes were driven into the ground at each end. The first pair was about a foot beyond the end of the gunwale and about 1½ inches apart. The second pair, similarly spaced, was about 6 inches beyond the first. Great care was taken to line up the last pair of stakes with the center line of the gunwale frame. The distance between these last stakes over the total gunwale frame was about 18½ feet.

The canoe builder now carefully inspected his gunwale frame and the staking. If he was satisfied, he then removed each stake and put it on the ground outside the building bed but near its hole. The weights were removed from the gunwale frame, which was also taken off the building bed. The bed was smoothed if it had been disturbed.

Now the birch bark was taken out of storage (usually in a nearby pool) and unrolled onto the bed with its white side up. To keep it flexible, it was moistened often during the building period. Usually the bark was long enough but often not wide enough. If it was too short, pieces could be added either at this time or later. If it was not wide enough, it was centered on the building bed, and the piecing was done later. The gunwale frame was then laid on the bark as close as possible to its original position.

The bark was then slashed from its outer edge to a point close to the end of each crosspiece. Another slash was made between each of these. All of the cuts were made to within about an inch of the gunwale except at the ends. As the cuts were made, the bark was bent slightly to put it under tension. Later, when the exact shape was determined, these slashes were gored or cut to make triangular pieces for precise fitting—that is, flush rather than overlapped. As the builder made the slashes, he also checked the bark for irregularities and often made his cuts so that blemishes would be trimmed out in the goring.

After the slashes were made, the bark was turned up carefully to expose the stake holes, and the stakes were replaced, the frame and the bark aligned again during the process. The longest stakes were put at the ends where the hull would be deepest. The tops of stakes directly opposite

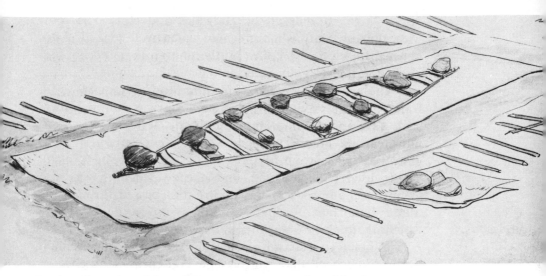

In second stage, stakes and frame were removed, and bark was rolled out on the building bed. Frame was then replaced over bark.

each other were then tied securely with thongs of bark to hold them straight and rigid.

At this point, it was obvious where more bark was needed to complete the width, and most builders did their piecing at this time. If the bark had to be lapped somewhere below the waterline, the pieces were first scraped thin on the edges so that no ridges would be formed where the two were joined, or the two pieces were joined carefully edge to edge. On laps above the waterline, the exposed edge was always positioned to the rear. If it was in the middle, the exposed edge was on top or toward the gunwale. With edge-to-edge joining, of course, it was not necessary to be concerned about the direction of the laps.

The ends of strands of roots used in lashing or sewing were sharpened so they could be fed through the awl holes more easily. For piecing, very small strands were generally used; larger strands at the gunwales and ends. The roots were flexible only when green or when well soaked. After drying, they became rather brittle, though they did not lose their holding strength. Some Indians used rawhide.

Indian women did the stitching, and they employed a variety of styles. Some of the stitching was simple, others elaborate and even decorative, generally following a pattern of a certain number of long stitches (each about 1 inch) followed by a group of short stiches (each about ½ inch). Some used cross-stitching, and harness stitching was also common, both ends of the sewing root passed through the same hole but in opposite directions. In double-thong stitching, the lacing was in-and-out from each side.

When a root strand was too short to complete a seam, it was tucked back under the last several turns or stitches on the inside and pulled tight. Similarly, the tail was tucked under the first stitch to keep it from pulling through. Bark near the middle got more stress than bark at the ends, and so the stitching here was very close and overlapped, usually so the stitches crossed the grain of the bark at an angle.

Types of stitching used by Indian women to sew bark.

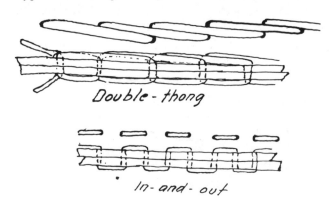

Double-thong

In-and-out

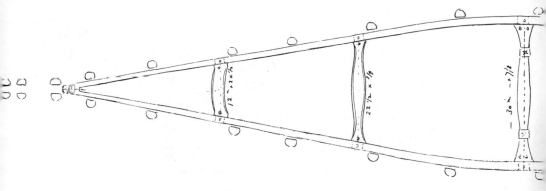

Position of gunwales, crosspieces, and stakes on building bed.

Sometimes lapped seams were also strengthened with a row of stitches parallel to those across the seam. A batten was generally used to back the seam during sewing so that the stitches could be pulled tight.

Bark was fastened to the gunwales either with continuous over-and-over stitches or with groups of lashings made through the same hole. The lashings were generally positioned between the rib heads, a measuring stick used to space them. If a strand was passed from one group of lashings to another, it was usually stitched under the gunwale to the new position. If each lashing group was independent, the tails of the lashing root were tucked under the last turns, generally on the inside of the gunwale. Some canoes had both inner and outer gunwales, the lashing going around both. If a cap was put over the gunwales, the lashing was done first so that the cap went over it.

With the piecing done, the bark was turned up around the gunwale frame and held in position there with small stakes. The bark was between the larger outer stake and the smaller inner stake, which was beveled at the lower end and fit against the gunwale. When the bark was firmly positioned,

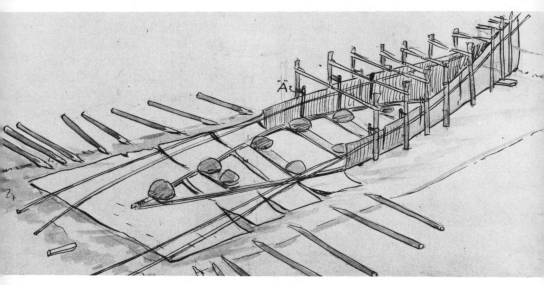

With gunwale frame in position, bark was sliced to crosspieces and then lifted so that stakes could be replaced in holes to establish frame of canoe.

At this stage, gunwale frame was lifted and positioned over stakes at ends of crosspieces.

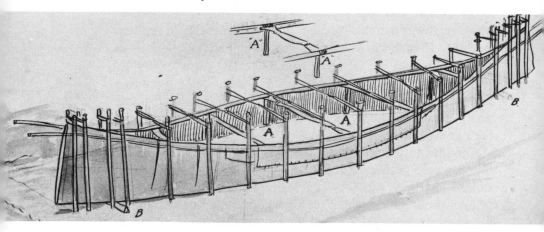

In top illustration, gunwale frame is still on bark, with weights on crosspieces. Below, frame has been lifted onto stakes, and weights have been replaced on pieces of wood laid across crosspieces.

the top of the stake was tied to the outer stake. Great care had to be taken that this inner stake did not puncture the bark. At the ends of the canoe, the large stakes were close enough together to hold the bark in position without smaller stakes. As the bark was lifted into position and secured, battens or strips were inserted along each side to help shape the sides.

After the sides were turned up and clamped in position, the slashes were gored so that the bark could be sewed together with edge-to-edge seams. Now the weights were removed from the gunwale frame to permit lifting the frame. If the building was done carefully, the frame could be lifted without disturbing the inside stakes, but it was usually necessary to loosen the ties across the outside stakes slightly. Short stakes of the proper length were already cut to fit under each crosspiece and also one for each end of the gunwale frame. For this canoe, the length of these stakes was 7½ inches for the middle crosspiece, 9 inches for the next crosspieces on each side, and 12 inches for the last crosspieces. Those at the gunwale ends measured 17 inches. The ends of these stakes were squared but smooth. When the gunwale was lifted, the stakes were put in position from the middle to the ends. Flat-sided pieces of wood were laid across each crosspiece and then rocks put on top of them to hold the gunwale frame on the posts.

If a canoe had only a single gunwale, the bark was now lashed or sewed to it. If a canoe was to have a double gunwale, it was now fit in position. Made of white cedar, about 19½ feet long, and rounded on the outer side, each was slid carefully between the bark and the outside stakes. The inside stakes were removed one by one as the outer gunwale was put in place. At 6- to 9-inch intervals from the middle to the last of the crosspieces, the two gunwales were pegged together with the bark between them. The pegs were made of ½-inch dowels sharpened at their ends and then driven into holes drilled into both gunwales. The pegs were cut off flush with the surface of the gunwales.

In a Malecite canoe, there were bark covers over the ends of the inner gunwales. These were put in position at this time so they could be held in position by the outer gunwale; the ends were forced inside the stakes beyond the ends of the gunwale. They were not cut at this time. Now the bark and the gunwales were lashed. Sometimes the bark was cut flush with the top of the gunwale, but many builders allowed the bark to turn down in a flap over the inner gunwale and then lashed over it. This made the lashing strong. In lashing, two or three turns of the root lacing were made through the same hole, resulting in a W-form and necessitating only two or three holes being made for each group of lashings. Care was taken to space the turns over the gunwale evenly and without overlaps. At the same time the crosspieces were also securely lashed to the gunwales.

Now the canoe could be lifted from the building bed and put at a more convenient height for working. The weights were removed, the stakes pulled, and the canoe turned upside down across logs anchored between boulders or over two crude log horses. At this stage the ends of the canoe could be closed. In the Malecite canoe, the stem pieces were made from two pieces of white cedar, each about 3 feet long and 1½ inches square. Each was shaped so that its outer face was only about half as wide as its inner face, thus forming a blunt-nosed triangle. Each piece was split into half a dozen laminations, the splits to within about 6 inches of the end that was to form the heel. The pieces were then soaked in boiling water to make them flexible for bending to form the curve of the stem. The bent pieces were held in place either with pegs or with root cords until dried, and then the laminations were wrapped tightly.

The ends of the outer gunwales were now cut to fit and were notched at their ends to receive the head of the stem piece. The stem was inserted between the bark ends of the canoe with the keel resting along the bottom for a short distance and the top at the desired height. Some builders allowed the outer gunwales to project beyond the stem, or they let the head of the stem project above the outer gunwale. This was a personal choice. To trim excess bark, one worker held the stem in place while the other trimmed.

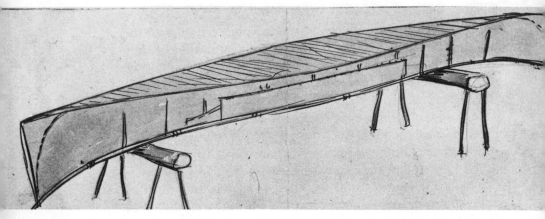

Canoe was lifted from building bed and turned upside down over log "horses," or boulders, to get convenient working height.

This firmed the end profile of the canoe. The bark was then lashed to the stem with a spiral stitching, the stitches close together and pulled tight to fit snugly. In places, the bark was trimmed a bit more to get an even closer fit. The ends of the outer gunwales were lashed tightly to each other, as well as to the bark.

All of the seams and the sewing were now given a final inspection before being sealed. The gum was heated and satisfactorily tempered, then spread into each seam and pressed into place with a thumb moistened with water to keep the gum from burning or sticking. When a seam had been filled, it was then covered with a thin piece of bark. As the builder worked, he examined the entire bark surface so that any holes or splits could be filled while the gum was ready.

Now the canoe was prepared for the ribs and sheathing on the floor and sides. The sheaths had been split in advance from white cedar. Each was 5 to 9 feet long, 3 to 4¼ inches wide, and about ⅛ inch thick. Their ends were whittled to a feather edge, the beveling started about 2 inches from the

Ribs were soaked in heated water, then bent into desired shape and held in that position with root ties or thongs until dried.

tips. Temporary ribs had also been made from flexible basket ash for holding the sheathing in place.

The permanent ribs—totaling about 50—were cut from white cedar. All were about ⅜ of an inch thick. Those for the middle were 3 to 4 inches wide; toward the ends, 2 to 2½ inches wide. There were five lengths. The first six pairs were long enough for the midsection of the canoe when bent— three ribs on each side of the center crosspiece, or thwart. Before bending, these were pieces about 5 feet long. Five pairs slightly shorter were made for the space between the middle and the second crosspiece on each side and another

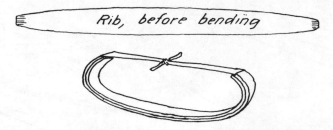

Rib, before bending

Above is a single rib before bending, and then after it is bent and tied to hold it in bent position for drying. Below are different ways sheathing was laid in canoes by different tribes.

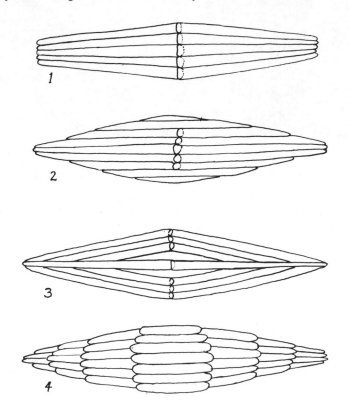

1

2

3

4

With bark sewed to frame, sheathing was placed on floor and sides of canoe. Then ribs were added to hold sheathing in place.

five pairs for the section between the next crosspieces on each side. Four pairs were made for the space between the last two crosspieces on each side; three pairs for the section around the end crosspiece; two or three pairs, much shorter, for use at or near the head pieces. Each rib was heated in boiling water and then bent over the knee or around a tree to a curvature slightly greater than needed. It was then tied with a thong to hold it in shape until it dried.

Sometimes ribs of green spruce were used. They were forced into approximate position against the bark and would "set" in this position as they dried. The bark was soaked with boiling water to make it flexible and elastic enough so that it would be bowed into the shape desired for the canoe by the ribs as they were put in place. To get the precise lengths needed for the ribs, measurements were made around the different sections of the canoe with a flexible root or with a piece of basket ash. Some builders used a measuring stick. The ribs were made a slight bit long to allow for a final fitting. In this case, as in all others in building the canoe, a considerable amount of judgment had to be exercised during the building, based on the materials and the particular circumstance.

With all the materials ready, the sheathing was now put in the canoe. In the Malecite canoe, the sheaths were laid lengthwise, the two pieces forming the full length overlapped by about 2 inches at the middle. The ends were narrowed so that they fit the tapering of the canoe and were slipped under the heel of the stem piece. After several were put in place, they were held there firmly with the temporary ribs. The bark was soaked with water again so that the sheathing could be curved up the side to give the canoe its slightly bellied shape. The final pieces were selected carefully to fit against the sewing of the bark at the gunwales.

The permanent ribs were now installed, a final measurement for their length taken with a root or with a piece of basket ash. A rib was set in place by slipping the ends under the gunwale on each side. It was driven into place to get a tight fit by placing a batten against the rib and then hitting it with a mallet. If the rib did not fit tightly enough to push the bark and make it taut, another rib was selected. Ribs slightly too short to be used in the middle could be used in some other place. If a rib was too long, even for the widest part of the canoe, it could be cut. All the while both the bark and the sewing had to be kept moist to make them elastic. Experience was valuable in knowing exactly how much pressure could be applied without breaking the bark. Achieving symmetry was also important. Sometimes a canoe was allowed to sit for a few days after the ribs were in place and then rechecked to correct any unevenness.

Headboards, each about 15¾ inches long, were made from a piece of white cedar about 4 inches wide and ¼ inch thick. The narrow end was cut off square, or nearly so, and the bottom was notched to fit the heel of the stem piece. The

Indian women gummed seams of canoes.

top was fit into a hole or notch gouged into the inner gunwales. The space between the stem and the headboard was stuffed with moss or cedar shavings to give the bow a firm and even shape. In tight fits, the board was put against the heel notch and then was bent slightly toward the worker so that it could be wedged into the place provided for it in the gunwale.

Two thin strips of white cedar, each about 19 feet long, were then made to cap the gunwales. Roughly ¼ inch thick, they were about 2 inches wide in the middle and tapered to an inch wide at their ends. These were laid on top of the inner gunwale and fastened there with wooden pegs. Their ends were usually lashed in position, in some cases worked into the lashings of the outer gunwale.

Now the canoe was turned upside down, and all of the outer seams were sealed with gum. The ends were generally gummed heavily and then also covered with a strip of thin bark. At the same time any holes or splits were repaired with gum as the worker checked the outer surface of the canoe. If the canoe was to be decorated (and not many were), the rough, reddish winter bark was scraped, leaving only the desired design.

Paddles were made of pieces of spruce, maple, ash, white cedar, or larch. Malecites made two types. One was long and narrow, the blade widest near the top and tapered to a narrow, rounded point. Above the widest point, the paddle narrowed quickly to a straight, slim handle, widened at the end for a hand hold. Another type was leaf-shaped or like a beaver's tail. In both, the blades were usually ridged down the middle.

Different builders used slightly different methods, and there were variations also in the techniques of different tribes in building canoes. Some used a special building frame for each size or model of canoe, replacing the use of the gunwale frame in the early stages of building the canoe. In some kinds, the building frame became a permanent part of the canoe. Some of the special styles and sizes of canoes built by the various tribes are described in the following chapters.

Canoes of the
Eastern Maritime Region

5   All of the tribes of Indians living in the eastern
coastal region of Canada and extreme north-
eastern United States were expert canoe builders.
It was their craft that were first seen by the
Europeans. The tribes in this area were the Malecite,
Micmac, Abnaki (a mixture of tribes), and Beothuk. Each
tribe built canoes of distinctive types to fit its special needs.

Malecite

These Indians lived originally in central and southern
New Brunswick and along the shore of Passamaquoddy Bay,
with subdivisions from the Penobscot to the Kennebec (these
later became part of the Abnaki). The Malecite were hunters
and warlike, generally friendly to the French but hostile to
the English.

The original Malecite canoes used in travel on large

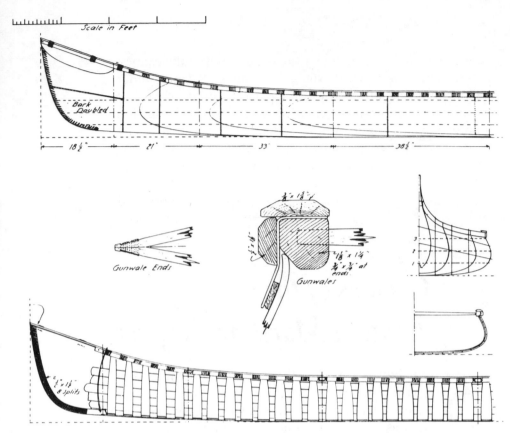

Construction details of a nineteenth-century Malecite 15-foot river canoe.

rivers and along the coast had high-peaked ends, curved strongly into the bottom. Small hunting canoes were similar but had a less abrupt lift at the ends. Canoes of this type were later replaced by models having rounded ends, the profiles practically a quarter circle. The Malecite war canoes were narrower than the regular hunting canoes; this made them faster for speedy travel to attack and to get away before pursuit parties could be organized. The war canoes were of standard length, however. They held only four warriors—two to paddle and two to use weapons while the canoe was still in the water. Usually the fighting was not done from the canoes, though. The Indians went ashore and fought on land. Under the gunwale near the ends was the personal mark of each of the four warriors, or if the canoe carried a tribal war leader, it bore only his mark. At the end of a raid, the Malecite warriors raced their canoes for the final mile or two home, and the winning canoe received some special mark to distinguish it.

On overnight trips the canoe was carried ashore and used as a shelter at night. The canoe was turned upside down, the tops of the ends resting on the ground. In the old high-ended canoes, it was only necessary to prop up one gunwale so that a man could crawl under the canoe for sleeping. With the low-ended canoes of later years, it was necessary to put props under the ends to lift the canoe high

A high-ended canoe used on large rivers, on lakes, and along coasts.

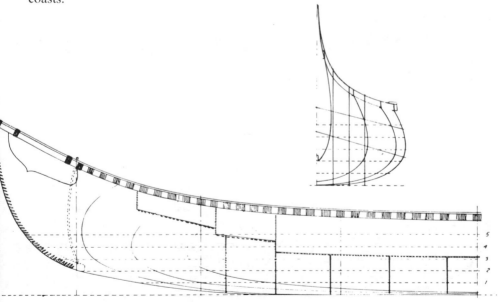

enough to get under. The forked sticks used as props were put on the end crosspieces. The dunnage (cargo) was stored under the ends of the canoe, and the two Indians then slept under a single blanket, their feet in opposite directions and their heads pillowed on part of the dunnage. If there were four men and the weather was bad, a crude shelter was made by laying poles across the canoe and then covering them with bark.

A Malecite racing canoe of the late nineteenth century. Note the decorations on the gunwales.

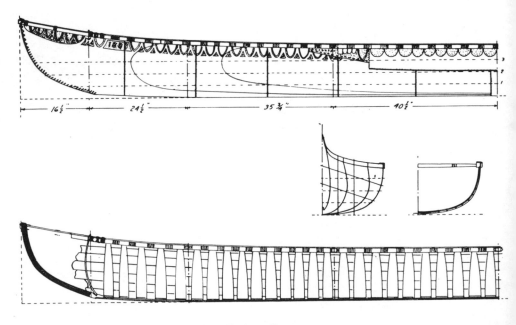

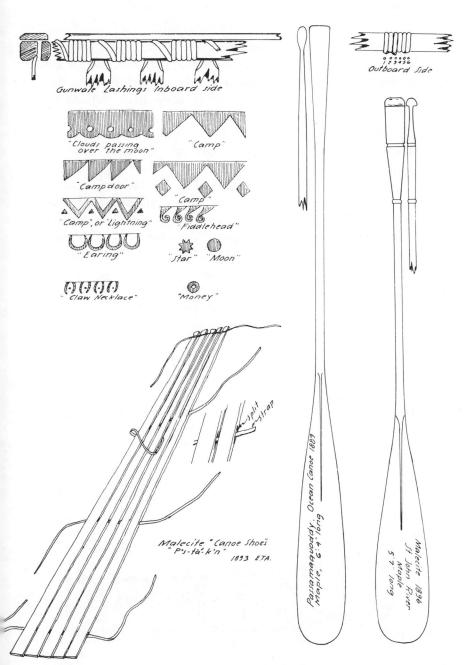

Gunwale Lashings Inboard side

Outboard Side

"Clouds passing over the moon"   "Camp"

"Campdoor"   "Camp"

"Camp" or "Lightning"   "Fiddlehead"

"Earing"   "Star"   "Moon"

"Claw Necklace"   "Money"

Split Strap

Malecite "Canoe Shoes" "Ps-tă-k'n" 1893 E.T.A.

Passamaquoddy, Ocean Canoe 1889 Maple, 6'4" long

Malecite 1896 St. John River Maple 5'7" long

Canoes of the Eastern Maritime Region   47

Before the snow was gone in spring, the Malecite sometimes hauled their canoes overland by mounting them on sleds or toboggans. If they used the canoes in fast water, they fastened splints of cedar together to make an outside sheathing for protecting the bark from rocks or snags. Two sets of these "canoe shoes" were made, the splints tied together with cords that were then brought up the sides of the canoe and tied to a crosspiece.

The Malecite were especially skilled at decorating their canoes. Sometimes they made their decorations by scraping the designs into the winter bark only along the gunwales, but often they decorated the entire canoe above the waterline. The owner's personal mark was placed near the ends. In some instances, the pictures on a canoe told a story. One side of the canoe, for example, might show a rabbit smoking a pipe, while the other side would have a picture of a lynx. In Malecite mythology, the rabbit was the ancestor of the tribe, and he was a great magician. The lynx was the rabbit's mortal enemy, but in the tribal tales, the rabbit always overcame the lynx by means of his magic. The canoe art

An old-style Malecite canoe with a high end and elaborate decorations.

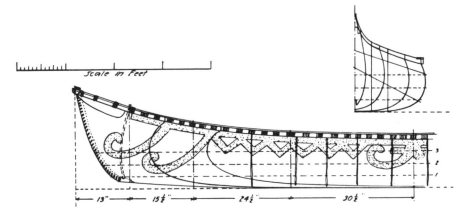

Scale in Feet

48   *How to Build an Indian Canoe*

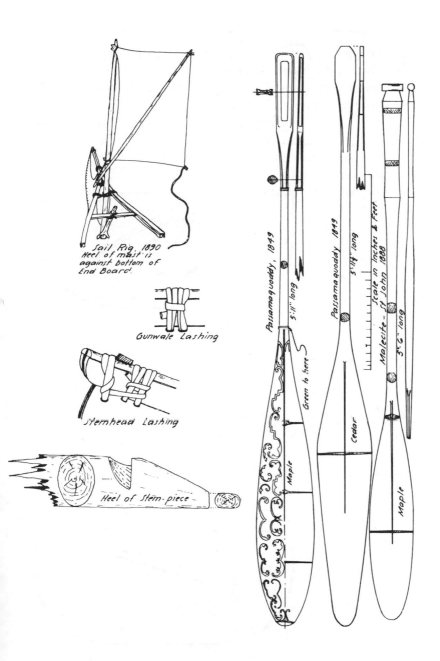

Sail Rig, 1890
Heel of mast is
against bottom of
End Board.

Gunwale Lashing

Stemhead Lashing

Heel of Stem-piece

Passamaquoddy, 1849

5'11" long

Green to here

Maple

Passamaquoddy, 1849

5'11½" long

Cedar

Malecite – St. John 1888

Scale in Inches & Feet

3'6" long

Maple

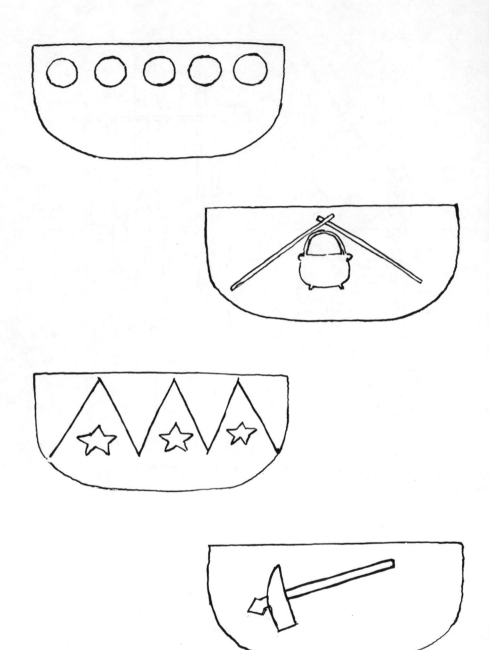

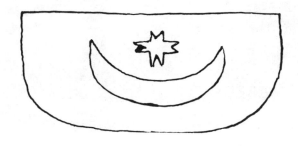

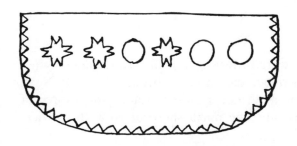

Some personal marks
used on canoe ends.

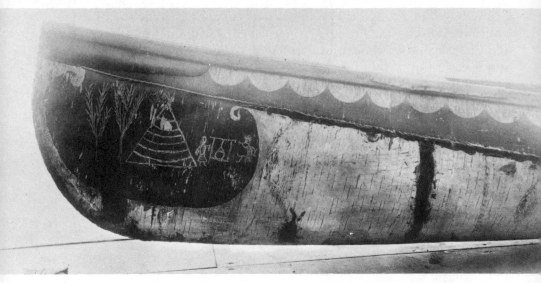

Canoe with rounded end and complete decorations.

depicted the rabbit sitting calmly smoking his pipe even though the lynx was near. The rabbit had confidence because he knew he could overcome the lynx.

Most of the designs on Malecite canoes were well proportioned and in good taste. Often a stencil was cut from birch bark so that a good design could be saved and duplicated time after time.

Malecite canoe builders were indeed fine craftsmen. They were perhaps the best of the birch-bark canoe builders.

Micmac

The Micmac were widespread in eastern Canada. When the Europeans arrived, the Micmac occupied all of Nova Scotia, Cape Breton, Prince Edward Island, the shores of the Bay of Fundy, and the north shore of New Brunswick.

They were hunters, and they were also warlike. They joined with the Malecite as allies of the French in warfare against the English. In the wooded, watery region where they lived, it was easiest to travel by canoe, and so they became experts at building canoes, producing them in several sizes and models.

The smallest, between 9 and 15 feet long, was the hunting canoe, also known as the woods canoe or the portage canoe. The big-river canoe was larger—between 15 and 20 feet long. Still larger was the open-water canoe, used for hunting seals and porpoises. It measured 18 to 24 feet long. War canoes, which presumably varied in length from 15 to 24 feet, were narrower so that greater speed could be achieved. All were well constructed, with a distinctive design. The bow and stern profiles were unlike those of any other tribe—almost circular and so streamlined that the ends flowed into the bottom line with almost no interruption. In the woods and river canoes, the gunwale line, or sheer, was almost straight. In the open-water canoe, it was 3 or 4 inches higher in the middle than at the ends, making a so-called hogged sheer. The hull was strongly bowed or bellied below the gunwale, giving the canoes much greater width or beam below the gunwales. In the woods canoes, the bottom was flat, in big-river canoes the bottom was rounded, and in open-water canoes it was rounded to slightly V-shaped.

All Micmac canoes had a very light build throughout. They did not, for example, have a framework to shape the ends; the stiffness needed there was achieved by putting battens on each side of the hull and lashing or sewing them in place with the bark. Sometimes additional battens, joined at the ends to those along the sides, were run from the high points of the ends to the last crosspieces. The gunwales were rarely more than 1¼ inches square, tapered slightly at the ends where they joined. The bark was always brought over the gunwale and folded down before being lashed. The cap for the gunwale was also thin—less than half an inch thick. The ends of the gunwales were supported by headboards made of hard maple, as were the crosspieces. The sheathing and ribs were of white cedar, the stem battens either of basket (black) ash or of spruce roots. The ribs were 3 inches wide at the bottom, tapering to 2 inches at their tops, and they were about ¼ inch thick.

Some of the open-water canoes were fitted for sailing. A guard strip was run the full length of the canoe on each side about 6 or 7 inches below the gunwale. This was to protect the strongly bowed out, or "tumble-home," sides from being abraded by the paddles, especially when the canoe was being steered under sail. The strips, about ¼ inch thick and ¾ inch wide, were lashed securely to the sides by stitches going completely around them and through the bark. The use of sails apparently came after the arrival of the white man, though it is believed that even earlier the Indians may have set up a leafy bush on the bow to act as a sail when winds were favorable. An old Nova Scotian expression of "carrying too much bush" refers to having too much canvas sail but is believed to have originated in those times when the Indians did actually use bushes. The Indians first used a simple square sail made either of bark or of moose hide. The use of canvas came later. They also adopted the spritsail, that is, a sail stiffened by a diagonal piece of wood or a sprit to which a cord was fastened so that the sail could be moved to catch the wind most advantageously. The sail's mast was attached to a crosspiece fastened to the gunwale caps.

The Micmac decorated their canoes by scraping away the inner rind of the birch bark, the design formed of the portions that were left. They apparently did little decorating until after their contact with the Malecite, and they never made elaborate or meaningful depictions. Their decorations

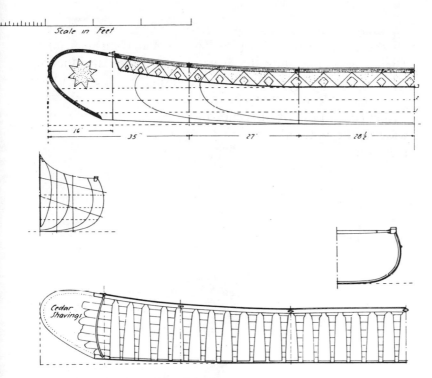

Mimac 2-fathom, or woods, canoe.

were simple, usually at the ends and in a long, narrow panel along the gunwale at midships. They were generally only of something that pleased the builder.

Because of their early contact with the Europeans, the Micmac soon lost much of their tribal craftsmanship in building canoes. Their construction methods deteriorated. They were the first of the Indians, for example, to use nails and tacks, which made the building faster but resulted in an inferior product.

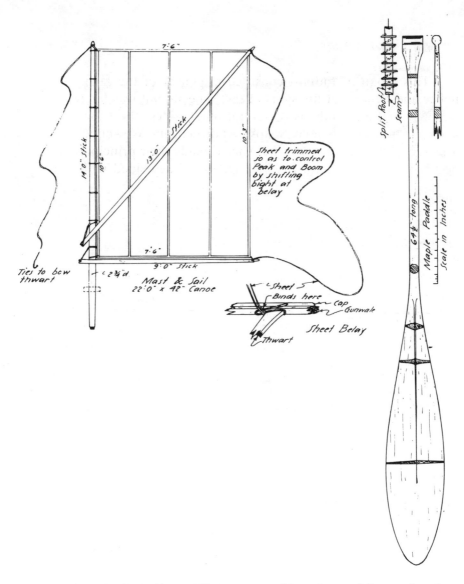

A spritsail used on a Micmac canoe. Note the cord fastened to the sail for moving it to catch the wind.

St. Francis-Abnaki

This group of Indians consisted originally of the Kennebec and Penobscot divisions of the Malecite but was later joined by refugee Indians of several other tribes—the Cowassek, Pennacook, Ossipee, Sokoki, Androscoggin, Wewenoc, Taconnet, and Pequawhet. The Abnaki made their principal home on the St. Francis River in Quebec. They sided with

St. Francis 2-fathom canoe of about 1865, with upright stems. Built for forest travel, this form ranged in size from 12 feet 6 inches overall and 26½-inch beam to 16 feet overall and 34-inch beam.

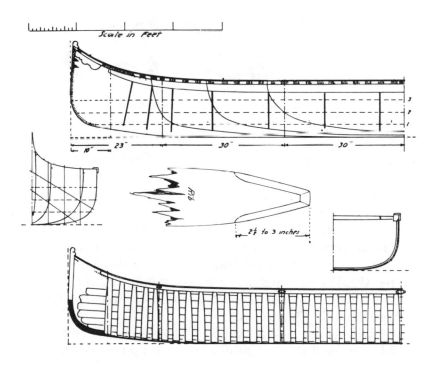

The Abnaki canoe incorporated ideas and techniques of various tribes.

the French and made many raids on English settlements. Often they carried white women and children home with them, and so they were soon a mixture of whites as well as of various Indian tribes.

The canoe developed by the Abnaki was basically of Malecite origin, but it had a distinctive design, incorporating some ideas obtained from Indians living farther to the west. The Abnaki canoe was thus a blend of different canoes, and it became the standard craft of travelers and sportsmen throughout the Quebec area.

The typical Abnaki canoe was high-ended, both bow and stern, and the end profiles were almost vertical. Some

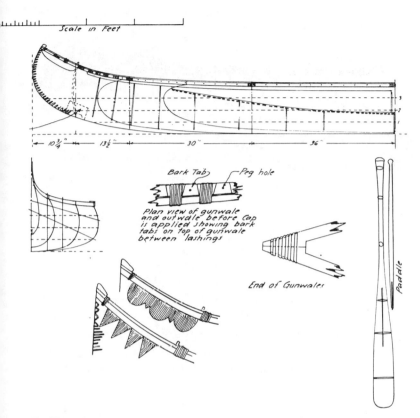

Scale in Feet

Bark Tab

Peg hole

Plan view of gunwale
and outwale before Cap
is applied showing bark
tabs on top of gunwale
between lashings

End of Gunwales

Paddle

St. Francis-Abnaki canoe for open water, a type that became
extinct before 1890.

were built also with a projecting "chin." Many of the woods
canoes were only 10 feet long, with a beam of 26 to 28 inches.
The popular length with sportsmen was 15 feet, with a beam
of 32 to 35 inches.

These canoes were built in almost the same way as were
those of the Malecite. Many did not have headboards,
however, and if one was used, it was narrow and was bowed
or bellied toward the end of the canoe. The sheathing was
cut in short lengths and laid in the canoe irregularly. The

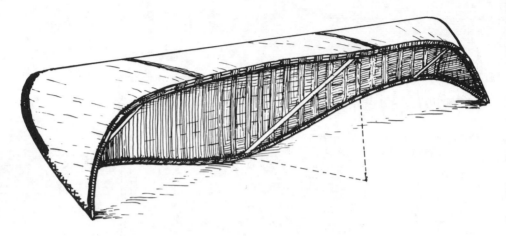

Beothuk canoes were distinctive because of their high ends. Most were also higher, or "hogged," at midships.

crosspieces, or thwarts, were spaced evenly along the length of the canoe rather than unequally as in Micmac and Malecite canoes. The ribs were bent green and held in place with battens and temporary crosspieces until they dried. They were then removed so that the sheathing could be added.

Beothuk

The Beothuk lived in Newfoundland and perhaps parts of Labrador. They were probably the first Indians contacted by the white man in northern North America. They were a small group, however, and were annihilated before 1800.

The canoes of the Beothuk were the most distinctive of those built by the coastal Indians, but details about how they were built are lacking. In cross section, the canoes were nearly V-shaped, which made them more seaworthy for travel in the coastal waters. They were, in fact, the only bark canoes that had a definite keel. (The Malecite made a keeled canoe of moose hide.) In their travel from island to island, the Beothuk presumably made trips on the open sea of fifty miles or more.

The gunwales of the Beothuk canoe were very high, or "hogged," at midships. This protected both the passengers and the cargo from spray in rough waters of the big rivers, bays, and coastal sea. Rock ballasts were probably added at both bow and stern. Protruding above each end was a separate stick that was used as a handle for carrying the canoe and also as a brace to support the canoe when it was turned over ashore for use as a shelter.

Canoes of Central Canada

6 This broad region includes what are now the provinces of Quebec, Ontario, Manitoba, and eastern Saskatchewan, plus northern Michigan, Wisconsin, and Minnesota in the United States. Most of the Indians living here belonged to the Algonkin family, but some members of the Iroquois Confederacy as well as Sioux, Dakota, Teton, and Assiniboni were also found here—particularly after trading with the French was begun. The tribes intermingled, and the canoes they built tended to be hybrids.

Eastern Cree

These Indians built so-called crooked canoes, that is, with a distinct rise of the bottom both fore and aft without a corresponding rise in the gunwale line, or sheer. As a result, the canoes were much deeper in the middle than at the ends. The Cree used a building frame rather than shaping the canoe around the gunwale for a frame, as the maritime Indians did. The building bed was lower in the middle rather than raised, and the building frame was bowed fore and aft to achieve the rockered bottom. It was necessary also to gore the bark at closely spaced intervals to form the sharply up-turned bottom.

Canoes with straight bottoms were also built by the Cree. For this style, the building bed was raised slightly in the middle, just as it was by the coastal Indians in building their canoes. To achieve the sharp rise at the ends, the building frame was bent up abruptly.

In both the crooked and straight-bottomed canoes, only a single gunwale was used, the bark lashed or sewed to it as in Malecite canoes. Sometimes a batten was placed under the

Montagnais crooked canoe.

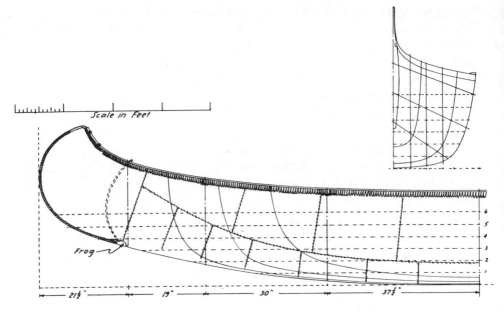

Scale in Feet

Frog

21½"   19"   30"   37½"

Crooked canoe, 2½-fathom, used by the Ungava-Cree, Montagnais, and Nascapee.

lashing to prevent the lashes from tearing out, and because good roots were not as available here as in the coastal areas, the Indians often used rawhide. The ends of the gunwales were supported by headboards that, in most canoes, were strongly bellied toward the ends. The ends were stiffened with outside battens rather than with stem pieces. At the top the battens were bent sharply to form a somewhat rounded peak where they met the gunwale caps.

The framework of the Cree canoe was usually made of spruce or larch, with white cedar employed in the southern part of the region and along the St. Lawrence River. The ribs were 3 inches wide, tapered to about 2 inches at the ends. At midships they were about an inch apart but were more widely separated toward the ends. The last three ribs at each

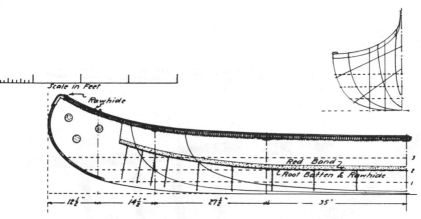

Montagnais 2-fathom canoe of Southern Labrador and Quebec, showing old-decoration form.

end were "broken" at the center to form a V shape there. Starting with the fourth rib from each end, the ribs were only sharply bent.

Straight-bottomed canoes were 12 to 18 feet long, with 14 to 16 feet the most popular. Crooked canoes, averaging 16 to 20 feet, were especially good for travel in open waters and in rapids. They were designed for carrying cargo rather than for use in hunting or in forest travel.

Têtes de Boule

Made up of bands of Indians inhabiting lower Quebec in the basin of the St. Maurice River, the Têtes de Boule were known to the Algonkins as "wild Indians." French traders called them "round heads" or "bull heads" because, unlike any of the other Indians in the North Country, they cut their hair short. The literal translation of their tribal name is White Fish People. The Têtes de Boule were skilled

Fiddlehead of scraped bark on bow and stern of a Montagnais birch-bark canoe at Seven Islands, Quebec, 1915.

canoe builders and were employed by the Hudson Bay Company to make their big canoes.

Canoes built by the Têtes de Boule resembled those made by the St. Francis-Abnaki but were narrower. Hunters' canoes measured 8 to 12 feet long; family canoes were longer—14 to 16 feet. They were straight across the bottom and then rose sharply at the ends. The stems bowed out or had a "chin," and the ends were given a V shape by breaking the end rib in the center. The sharpened end made the canoe cut through the water more easily and made paddling less difficult. The Têtes de Boule did not ordinarily decorate their canoes, but they did add decorations to those they built for the white man. Their paddles were similar to those used by the Cree but were slightly wider toward the tip. The top grip was wide and thin. Usually the paddles were made of white birch, but maple was also used.

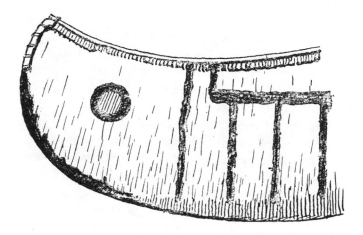

Disk of colored porcupine quills decorating canoe found at
Namaquagon, Quebec, 1898 . . . Têtes de Boule hunting canoe,
1½-fathom.

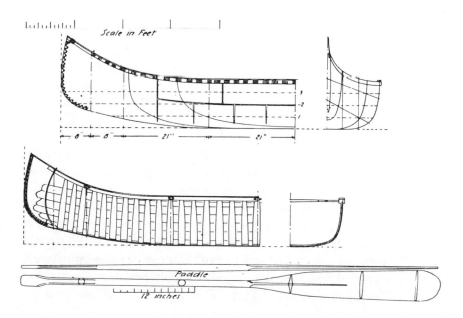

Algonkin

The Algonkin, a large and powerful tribe, lived on the Ottawa River and its tributaries in Quebec and Ontario. They participated strongly in the fur trade with the French, for whom they also made canoes, and they also intermingled with tribes of the Iroquois Confederacy. As a result of these various contacts, their canoes were hybridized.

The oldest type known had high ends, a narrow bottom, and flaring sides. Built with careful workmanship, it was lightweight and easily paddled. The bottom was straight, lifted only slightly at the sharp ends. The line of the gunwales, or sheer, was almost straight over most of the length of the canoe, then lifted sharply near the stem and became almost perpendicular. The stem piece was built so that it ended in a straight line across the sheer, or line of the gunwale. These high-ended canoes were built in lengths from 14 to 16 feet.

The Iroquois living in Algonkin territory built a 12- to 18-foot canoe that was similar to Malecite and Abnaki canoes but with a narrower bottom and flaring sides. Most of them had high-peaked ends like the canoes of the Abnaki, but one type had exceptionally low ends. These were obviously copies of the canoes built by the coastal Indians, and the same building methods were employed. The Algonkins always used a building frame, however, and they built their canoes on a level building bed in which a 6-inch-wide board 6 to 8 feet long was sunk in the earth flush with the surface. This was to assure a true line for the bottom.

Like the Têtes de Boule, the Algonkins built canoes that were not as deep at midships as were those of the coastal Indians, who used their craft in rougher, more open water. The stem pieces of later types of Algonkin canoes protruded above the gunwales. These canoes, called wabinaki chiman, were often decorated, but the figures used apparently had no

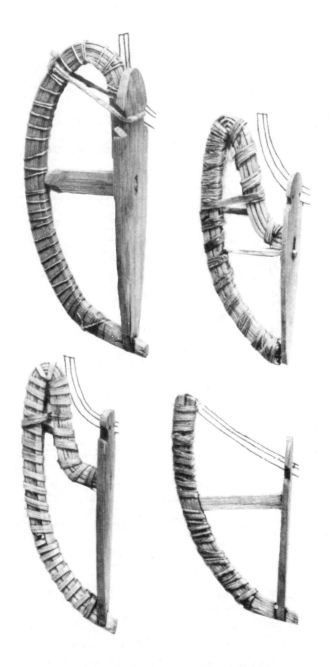

Styles of stem pieces used by Algonkin and Ojibway.

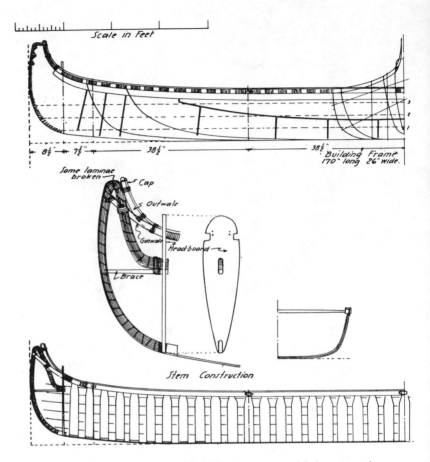

Scale in Feet

Building Frame
170" long 26" wide.

Some laminae
broken
Cap
Outwale
Gunwale
Headboard
Brace

Stem Construction

Old model, Ottawa river, Algonkin canoe, combining capacity
with easy paddling qualities.

mythological significance and were selected only because
they appealed to the builder.

In portaging, the Algonkins put a pair of paddles a foot
or so apart just in front of and just behind the middle
crosspiece, lashing them securely in place with bark or
rawhide. The canoe was lifted and turned over so that the

paddle handles fit on the carrier's shoulders. A loop of the bark or hide was put over the carrier's forehead so the canoe could not slip backward. The band around the carrier's forehead was called a tump line. Other heavy loads were also carried with a harness and tump line arrangement.

Algonkin canoe decorations by Tommy Sersin, Golden Lake, Ontario, showing four sides of stems of one canoe.

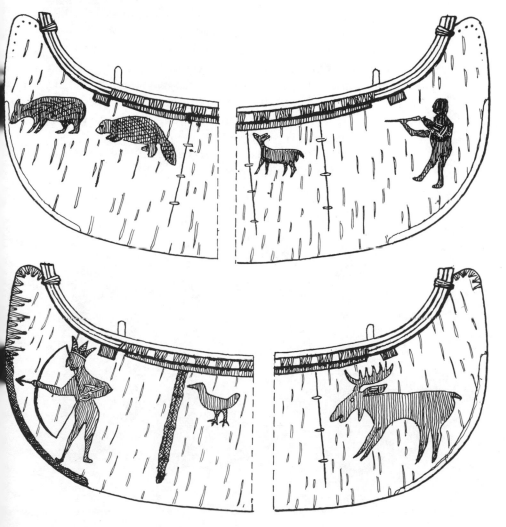

Ojibway

The Ojibway lived all around Lake Superior. With the Western Cree, they pushed the Sioux westward into the plains, but in the process they also absorbed some of the Sioux and the Cree into their own tribe. In this large tribal group were such bands as the Chippewa and Menominee. All were expert canoe builders, and they modified their basic tribal canoe form to incorporate desirable features of other canoes. The original Ojibway canoe was probably a high-ended type, much like the Algonkin but of larger size.

All of the Ojibway canoes were constructed by using a building frame, and the building bed was higher in the middle than at the ends. The most common type used west and northwest of Lake Superior was the "long-nose" canoe, which had especially high ends. The end profile was rounded; however, the "chin" projected a foot or more beyond the end of the gunwales.

Ojibway stem pieces.

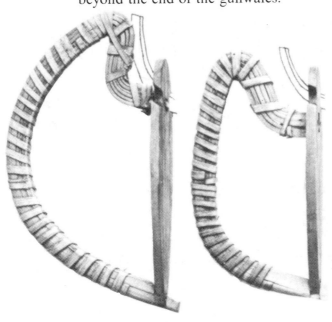

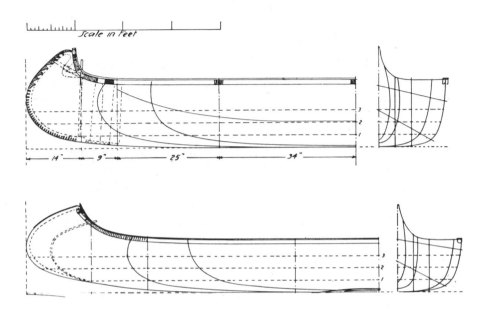

Ojibway "long-nose" canoes in two styles. Note long "chins."

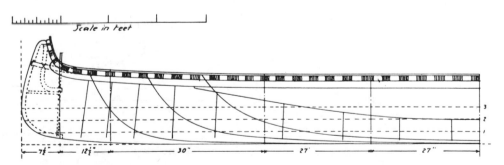

An 18-foot rice-harvesting canoe.

Western Cree

The western division of the large Cree tribe lived in northern Ontario, northern Manitoba north of Lake Winnipeg, and northwestern Alberta. Their canoes were similar to the long-nosed Ojibway canoes but had a less pronounced, less rounded chin and also less rocker at the ends. Because birches were scarce in this region, the Western Cree often used spruce bark—with good results. If they could not get good roots, they made their lashings with rawhide.

Western Cree 2½-fathom canoe, built of either birch or spruce bark. Inside root stem piece, round gunwales, and much-bellied headboard are typical.

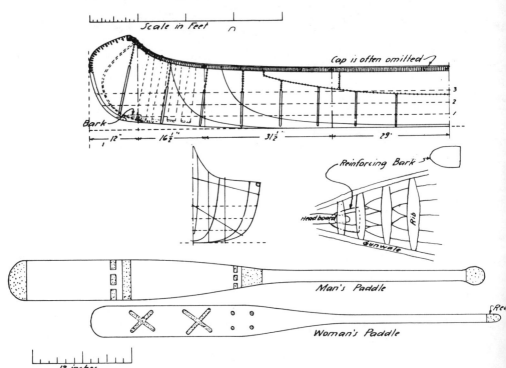

Canoes of
Northwestern Canada

7 Indians living in extreme northwestern Canada and in what are now the states of Washington and Alaska built three basic types of bark canoes. In this region, paper birch trees were not abundant, and they were also smaller and produced bark of inferior quality. Many of the canoes, as a result, were made of spruce bark, and some tribes used seal skins or other hides.

One of the types of canoes built by these Indians was the "kayak" model—a flat-bottomed, low-sided and partly decked narrow canoe. A number of tribes constructed canoes of this sort, and most of the same tribes also built a narrow-bottomed canoe with flaring sides and high ends. The kayak type was used for hunting, and the narrow-bottomed canoe was for the family or for hauling cargo. The sturgeon-nose canoe, a third type, had the ends projected into a long, pointed "ram" as an extension of the bottom. This type was built only in a limited area of British Columbia. Most of the canoe builders of this region belonged to the Athabascan family. Included were the Chipewyans, Dogrib, Slave, Beaver, Tanana, Loucheux, Hare, and others.

Kayak-type canoe

This canoe was highly developed in the Northwest. The canoes used for hunting ranged in length from 12 to 18 feet and had a beam of 24 to 27 inches. If the kayak was to be used also for family transportation, it was longer—to 25 feet—and had a beam of about 20 inches. In most, the greatest beam width and also the greatest depth of the canoe was just behind the middle. Cargo or family canoes had no decking, but the shorter hunting canoes were decked, mostly in the front. The end profile of the kayak-type canoes differed with each tribal group, and were identifiable. In most, the bow and stern were also distinct. Kayak-type canoes characteristically had a slightly bowed, or "hogged," bottom, which was not evident when the canoe was afloat. In most of these canoes, the paddler sat on a sheet of bark that was attached to the bottom. The paddles were mostly single-bladed, with parallel sides, but tapered to a point or a rounded tip. Some ended in a knob; others had a cross-grip handle. A few paddles had double blades like those used in the Alaskan sea kayaks.

Narrow-bottom canoe

Built extensively by the Chipewyans, Dogrib, and Slave tribes, this type of canoe was of Algonkin-Ojibway origin. It measured 16 to 22 feet in length and had a beam of 36 to 48 inches. The bottom was straight, or there was only a moderate turning up at the ends, which were not high. The

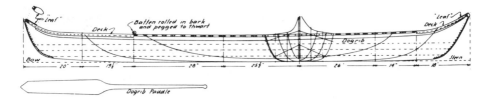

Athabascan kayak-style hunting canoe.

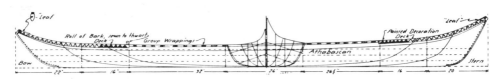

Kayak-style canoe of Alaskan Eskimo.

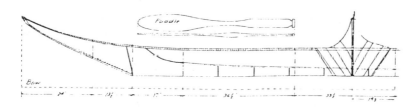

Kayak-style canoe used in British Columbia.

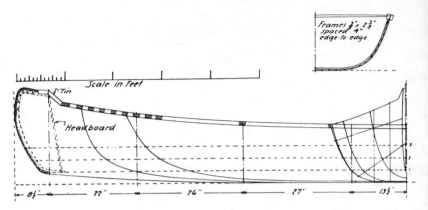

Athabascan cargo or family canoe with bent stem pieces,
Chipewyan 2½-fathom. This canoe was covered with spruce or
birch bark.

end profiles varied with the tribe. Those built by the
Chipewyans had a long end profile both fore and aft. Dogrib
canoes had a similar but deeper profile, appearing much
higher than they really were. The large Slave canoes had
ends formed of a thin plank, slightly curved but almost
vertical.

On open water, these canoes were fitted with a square
sail—usually made of a blanket. A temporary mast of a
sapling was mounted in a hole in the second crosspiece.

Sturgeon-nose canoe

Ram-ended or sturgeon-nose canoes were constructed
by Indians living in southern British Columbia and in
northern Washington. They differed greatly from the canoes
built by any other North American Indians, resembling more
nearly a similar kind of craft built in Asia. Sturgeon-nose
canoes were built by Indians of the Kutenai and the Salish
groups. They were made of birch, spruce, fir, pine—whatever

kind of bark was available. Their distinctive feature was the long ram-ended profile, the stem profile angling out to the "nose" in a nearly straight line. No stem pieces were used, and the bark ends were closed with battens attached to the outside and extending about 3 inches above the gunwales. The bottom was either straight or slightly bowed, or "hogged," exaggerated considerably after the canoe was used for a while in hauling cargo. The workmanship was good.

These canoes paddled well in strong winds and in rough water. They could be worked quietly in the marshes, where they were commonly used in hunting.

Bark canoe of the Kutenai and the Shuswap.

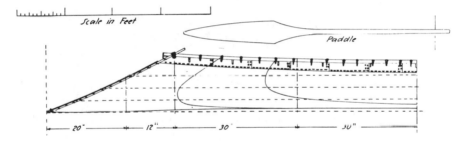

Fur-Trade Canoes

8 The most famous of all the birch-bark canoes were those used by the French fur traders. Also called *canots du maître, maître canots, rabeskas,* or great canoes, these big canoes saw nearly two centuries of use. Without them there would have been no Canadian and American fur trade. In addition to playing a vital role in this exploitation of one of the continent's richest resources, the canoes made possible the exploration and settlement of the North Country. They can be compared in their importance and contribution to such other vehicles of travel in settling and expanding North America as covered wagons, locomotives, and steamships.

It is believed that the earliest of the fur-trade canoes were developed from Algonkin-type high-ended canoes, but over the years they were variously modified to take advantage of whatever good features the builders could incorpo-

The great canoes of the fur traders were built for speed and for carrying heavy cargoes.

rate. Standard models were produced in a canoe factory set up at Trois Rivières.

All of the fur-trade canoes had narrow bottoms, flaring topsides, and sharp ends. They were designed to carry heavy cargoes with speed. On the Montreal–Great Lakes run, the fur-trade canoes were commonly 36 feet in overall length—32 feet 9 inches along the gunwales and 32 feet along the bottom. They averaged 5½ feet in beam width, some to almost 6 feet. At midships, they were 30–32 inches deep, and they were 54 inches high at the stem. This giant was later replaced with a canoe about 31 feet long, 5 feet in beam width, 30 inches high at midships, and 50 inches high at the stem. Some of the express canoes were only about 20 feet long.

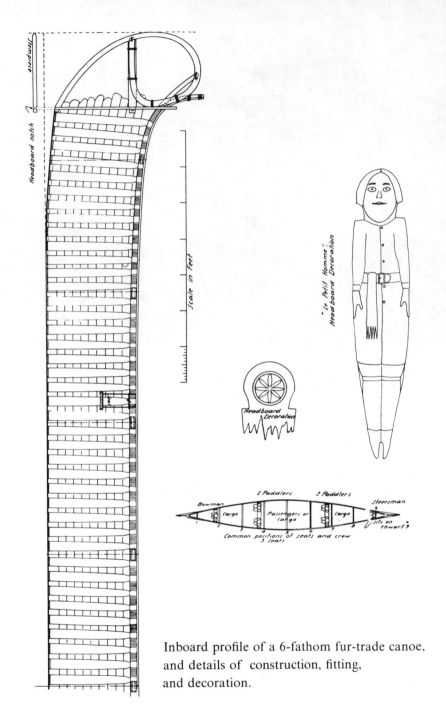

Inboard profile of a 6-fathom fur-trade canoe, and details of construction, fitting, and decoration.

82   *How to Build an Indian Canoe*

Fur-trade canoes carried their cargo in bundles that weighed 90 to 100 pounds. The furs were packed by using screw presses, so that 500 mink skins could be compressed into a 90-pound package that measured only 24 x 21 x 15 inches. In the canoe these packs were covered with an oiled red canvas tarp to protect them. Liquor and wine was carried in 9-gallon kegs, the least manageable of the cargo. The fur traders also carried boxes, or cassettes, that were 28 inches long and 16 inches wide and deep. Strapped with iron and with a tightly fitting lid held shut with a padlock, the cassette was made as watertight as possible. Each was painted and marked, and inside, the traders stored their cash and other valuables. One cassette contained medicines and refreshments. Meat, sugar, flour, and other food items were stowed in tins and put in pack baskets, as were the cooking utensils and any other loose articles. Bedrolls and clothing were rolled in a tarp or in an oilskin ground cloth.

Packages ready for portage, called a pacton, were usually combined in groups of two for a total weight of about 180 pounds. No self-respecting voyageur would carry less than two packages, and to do so, he used a tump line or colliers, just as in portaging canoes. The tump line was made of broad bands of stout leather. The middle piece that fit around the head was about 4 inches wide and 18 inches long. It was attached to two flexible straps, 2–2½ inches wide and 10 feet long. Loads for most voyageurs were 3 pactons, or about 270 pounds, with a record of 630 pounds. The carrier moved at a trot, traveling about 5 miles per hour on a good trail.

A voyageur's life was not at all as carefree and adventuresome as is commonly depicted. He ate poorly, carried loads so heavy they caused him physical injury, and was exposed to the extremes of weather. He worked hard and lived a short life.

On their way to get furs, the traders carried a variety of supplies. For example, this was the cargo on a Red River run:

general merchandise, 5 bales	lead shot, 2 bags
tobacco, 1 bale and 2 rolls	flour, 1 bag
kettles, 1 bale	sugar, 1 keg
guns, 1 case	gunpowder, 2 kegs
hardware, 1 case	wine, 10 kegs

In addition, the canoe carried 4 bales of personal items, one for each of the four paddlers. Each also had 4 bags of corn (1½ bushels for each), ½ keg of cooking lard, plus bedrolls and canoe gear.

Items commonly used in trade with the Indians included awls, axes, shot, gunpowder, gun tools, brass wire, flints (and later, percussion caps), lead, beads, brooches, blankets, combs, coats, firesteels, finger rings, guns, spruce gum, garters, birch bark, powder horns or cartridge boxes, hats, kettles and pans, knives, fish line, hooks, net twine, looking glasses, needles, ribbons, rum, brandy, wine, broadcloth, tomahawks or hatchets, tobacco, pipes, thread, and dyes.

On most trips, the voyageurs averaged 50 miles a day, though this varied with the waterway and also the condition of the men. Express canoes sometimes covered as much as 80 miles per day, but that was exceptional. Some of the very large canoes had as many as 17 paddlers and a steersman, but usually there were fewer. The express canoes were manned by 6 or fewer.

Most of the fur-trade canoes were built specifically for the Hudson Bay Company, and under their supervision, though the actual building was done by the Indians. The builders used their judgment, suiting general directions but following no specific rules or regulations. Their decorations,

"Bivouac in Expedition in Hudson's Bay Canoe." From an oil painting by Hopkins.

if any, were not standardized, the builders either adding what they personally thought would be attractive or using whatever designs were customary for the trading post for which the canoe was being built. Some of the trading posts took special pride in the appearance of their canoes and had them painted with bright colors.

The building methods employed combined the techniques of the Algonkin and the Ojibway. At large trading posts, there were often several building beds, and canoes were under construction at all times. A building frame was always used, its length corresponding to the bottom length of the canoe.

Despite their large size, the express canoes were usually

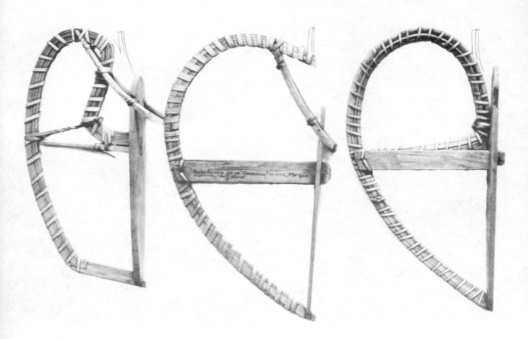

Stem pieces used on fur-trade canoes.

lightweight enough for two men to carry them. The big canoes required at least four men. The canoes were carried either in an upright position or upside down with the canoe supported on the carriers' shoulders.

Voyageurs were particular about their paddles. The blade was never wider than 5 inches, for wider blades made the paddling too difficult. In length, the paddles reached the user's chin when he stood with the blade on the ground and the handle up. The bow and stern men, the most skilled and also the highest paid of the voyageurs, used slightly longer paddles. These men also carried spare 8-foot paddles for steering when the canoe was running a rapids. The paddles were made of maple or some other hardwood, because these woods could be pared to thinner blades without loss of strength.

During the fur-trading season, brigades of big canoes moved along the waterways of the North Country. Those going the greatest distance left the trading post first, followed by brigades with shorter trips. The timing was carefully calculated so that all of the runs could be made and the canoes home again before winter set in.

The disappearance of the birch-bark canoe came gradually as canvas and wooden boats replaced it and as the fur trade itself declined in importance. The era of the big canoes ended just before World War I, the canoes becoming only talked-about giants of the past. Not even one of the big canoes was saved for display in a museum.

End decorations on fur-trade canoes.

Index